Teachable Moments

COOKBOOKS
FOR KIDS

Holidays and Special Days!

Brenda C. Ward
Jane Cabaniss Jarrell

WORD Kids!

WORD PUBLISHING
Dallas·London·Vancouver·Melbourne

Photography   Donald Fuller

Design   Sabra Smith

Managing Editor   Laura Minchew

Project Manager   Beverly Phillips

Food Styling   Jane Jarrell

Teachable Moments Cookbooks for Kids
Holidays and Special Days!

LIBRARY OF CONGRESS CATALOGING-IN-PUBLICATION DATA

Ward, Brenda.
Holidays and Special Days!/Brenda C. Ward, Jane
Cabaniss Jarrell.
   p.   cm.—(Teachable moments cookbooks for kids)
ISBN 0–8499–3673–1
1. Holiday cookery. I. Jarrell, Jane Cabaniss, 1961–   .
II. Title. III. Series.
TX739.W37   1995
641.5'68—dc20   95–11647
                                                          CIP

Printed in the United States of America
95 96 97 98 99   RRD   9 8 7 6 5 4 3 2 1

To Elizabeth Dillon,

for her legacy of faith.

And to the new generation of "angel babies"—

Margaret, Ashley, Jamie Lee, Dakota, Caleb,

Benjamin, Aaron, Laura Beth, Samantha, and Amy.

B . C . W .

To my husband Mark, a true love worth waiting for.

A special thanks to Deborah Saathoff and Cindy Hallmark for their help
with recipe testing and photography set-up.

J . C . J .

Contents

How to Use This Book
A Guide for Parents

Face it—parenting is hectic. Add the responsibility of teaching our children all the values and principles we as parents want to pass on, and you've gone from hectic to one huge guilt trip! Exactly when—between soccer, birthday parties, ballet, and softball—is there time to teach our children all the priceless principles they will need to hold in life?

The *Teachable Moments Cookbooks for Kids* are designed to help solve this problem by providing children and parents with natural teaching and learning times through an activity children love—cooking! Teachers have known for years that cooking is a wonderful vehicle for teaching. It reinforces math and language skills, and it encourages organization and sequential thinking. Best of all, it is a fun learning experience for children.

To make the most of the recipes and activities in this book, try the following helpful suggestions:

Have a PLAN:

❦ Decide what value you would like to cover with your children and look under that particular section in the book. Check the parties in that section to find the one that best fits your needs.

❦ Read the suggested recipe to determine how many children are appropriate for that particular activity. If inviting more than four to five children, consider asking one of their parents to come along and help.

❦ Plan ahead on the family parties, too. Pick a time of the week that is the least busy and stressful for everyone. Plan on a relaxing, fun time.

❦ Check recipes to make sure you've allotted enough preparation time. Some steps may need to be done the day before in order to finish the recipes in the length of time you have (for example, cookie dough that needs to chill for several hours).

Don't forget to PREPARE:

Things you'll need:

- wooden spoon
- knife
- saucepan

Sample of a "Things you'll need"

- Use the **Things you'll need** box *(see example on right)* and **Ingredients** section as easy references for setting up cooking trays ahead of time. Allow the children to pour, measure, and chop, but have all ingredients and equipment set up ahead of time.

- Advance preparation that needs to be done by you, such as browning meat or chopping onions, should be done ahead of time.

- Prepare a safe cooking environment for the children. Seated around a large table works great, but seated on a stool next to the stove is dangerous! Many schools use individual heating units in their cooking activities, and you may find that one would be well worth the investment. For best results, plug the cord in on the side of the table where you are sitting, and have the children work opposite you.

- Discuss rules for safety and sanitation before you begin any part of the activity, while you still have the children's total attention!

Remember the PURPOSE:

- Read or have children read the text as you begin each activity.

- Check the **Teachable Moments** box *(see example on left)* that is included for each activity to give you suggestions on how to make the most out of each one. Read the box ahead of time and remember the objective of each activity as you do it with the children.

- Sure, it's easier to prepare these foods yourself, but don't forget the long-term goal—you are passing on critical values to your children.

Teachable Moments

There are many ways you can help your children show their love for their mother. One great way is by helping the children make a coupon book. Coupons can be good for "one free room cleaning without complaining," "an undisturbed Saturday morning," or "a night out with friends, without coming home to a messy house!"

Teachable Moments information box

Sample of a value teaching from one of the cooking activities.

Have you ever had a person do something especially nice for you? Maybe a grandparent sent you a little gift when it wasn't even your birthday. Or a friend helped you clean your room so you could spend time together. The good feeling that you had toward the person who did something nice for you was thankfulness.

Thankfulness

is appreciating what others do for you. It can also mean being grateful for the good things you have been given by God. Food, clothes, a place to live, and people who love you are all things for which you might be thankful.

Being thankful isn't always as easy as it sounds. You may be used to having plenty of everything you need. It may seem natural to you to have people nearby who love you and take care of you. It can be hard not to take these things for granted, or just assume you should have them. Sometimes you may just wish you had a little more. You may think about all you *don't* have instead of remembering all you *do* have. When it comes to being thankful, what matters the most is to remember how much you do have and to have a thankful heart. Recognize what others do for you and all that you've been given—and express your thanks often!

Thanksgiving

 IT'S GREAT TO remember to be thankful every day, but there is one day each year when we pay special attention to thankfulness. This day is Thanksgiving.

The first Thanksgiving Day was celebrated in 1621. A group of people called Pilgrims had left their homes in England because they couldn't worship God in the way they wanted to. They came to America. Their first year in the new land was very difficult, and many of the Pilgrims died. But with the help of the Indians, the Pilgrims learned how to survive in the new land. The Indians taught them how to plant and fertilize corn, to dry fruit, to hunt wild animals, and to catch fish. The year ended with a good harvest, and the Pilgrims proclaimed a feast of thanksgiving for the harvest. They invited the Indians to the feast to show their appreciation and thankfulness for the Indians' help in keeping them alive.

Today, many people celebrate Thanksgiving Day by getting together with family or friends. It is a day to recognize all of the good things, or blessings, that we have in our lives, and to offer prayers of thanks for those blessings.

When we think of Thanksgiving, we usually think of turkey, cranberries, and pumpkin pie. But there was one food served at the first Thanksgiving that the Pilgrim children especially liked. The Indians brought corn, heated it in earthen jars, and made the first popcorn! Maple syrup was poured over the popcorn to make something similar to the popcorn balls we eat today.

This Thanksgiving, make these fun Maple Popcorn Balls and think about that first Thanksgiving feast. As you make the popcorn balls, think of the many reasons you have to be thankful. Like the Pilgrims and Indians many years ago, you can give thanks, too.

Popcorn on the Stove

Things you'll need:

large pot with lid

measuring cups

Ingredients:

½ cup popcorn
¼ cup vegetable oil
salt
butter

1. Place popcorn and oil in a large pot; move the pot around to distribute the oil.

2. Cover and cook on medium high heat until a few kernels pop.

3. Remove from heat for one minute.

4. Return to heat, shaking pan frequently until the popcorn stops popping. Add salt and butter to taste.

Makes about 8 cups popped popcorn.

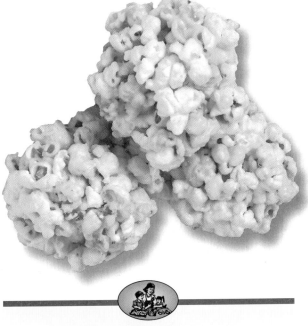

Teachable Moments

To make the most of this recipe, cook the popcorn over the stove. Tell the story of the first Thanksgiving, emphasizing that even though the Pilgrims had very few comforts and their lives were very difficult, they still offered prayers of thanks for all that they had.

Maple Popcorn Balls

Things you'll need:

- measuring cup
- measuring spoons
- double boiler
- spoon
- large bowl
- wax paper

Ingredients:

½ stick butter (4 tablespoons)
25 large marshmallows
1 teaspoon maple extract
8 cups popped popcorn

1. Place water in the bottom saucepan of a double boiler and place the second saucepan on top.

2. Melt butter and marshmallows in the top saucepan over medium heat. Stir in maple extract.

3. Place the popcorn in a large bowl that has been sprayed with cooking spray. Pour marshmallow and butter mixture onto the popcorn and stir thoroughly to combine.

4. Form into balls about three inches in diameter and place on wax paper to harden.

Makes 8 to 10 popcorn balls.

WHEN YOU THINK about people you are thankful for, you usually think about your family and friends. But have you stopped to think about other people who help you every week or even every day? Many teachers, coaches, and club leaders spend time helping others to learn, achieve, and have fun. It's important to recognize these people who help you learn and grow.

The Thanksgiving season is a perfect time to show these people you appreciate them. Make these Gobble-Gobble Cakes as a special "thank-you." Wrap each one in colored plastic wrap and tie it with a ribbon. For each person, include a note that says "I'm thankful for you because..." and fill in the blank. They will love to know you appreciate them!

Teachable Moments

Because children learn best by example, add to your child's note a short line of thanks from you, and read the message to her.

13

Gobble-Gobble Cakes

Things you'll need:

- measuring cups
- measuring spoons
- sifter
- 2 large bowls
- electric mixer
- plastic wrap
- rolling pin
- turkey-shaped cookie cutter
- cookie sheet
- spatula
- small clean paint brushes

Ingredients:

5¼ cups all-purpose flour, sifted
½ teaspoon baking soda
1 cup (2 sticks) butter, softened
3 cups sugar
3 eggs
food coloring (optional)
1 cup heavy cream

1. In a large bowl, sift together flour and baking soda and set aside. If you don't want to mess up another bowl, sift flour and soda onto wax paper.

2. In a large bowl, cream the butter.

3. Gradually add sugar and beat on low speed for two minutes.

4. Add the eggs one at a time, beating after each addition until thoroughly mixed.

5. If coloring the dough, add food coloring to the cream prior to stirring it into the flour.

6. Add the flour mixture, alternating with the cream. Beat only until smooth after each addition.

7. Divide dough into quarters and wrap each part tightly in plastic wrap. Refrigerate overnight.

8. Preheat oven to 350 degrees.

9. Using a floured rolling pin, roll out each part of the dough to a thickness of about ¼ inch on a floured surface. Cut into turkey shapes using a cookie cutter.

10. Place dough shapes on a cookie sheet and bake for 15 minutes, or until lightly browned.

11. Using a spatula, remove cookies from cookie sheet and let them cool.

12. Paint turkeys with icing, using clean paint brushes.

Makes 3 to 4 dozen.

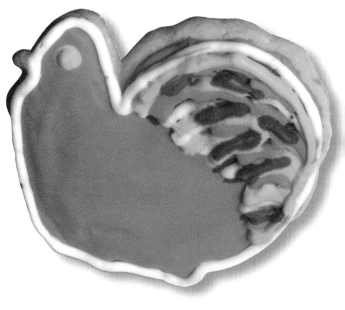

Gobble-Gobble Cakes Icing

Things you'll need:

- sifter
- small bowl
- measuring cup
- measuring spoons
- spoon
- clean paint brushes

Ingredients:

2 cups powdered sugar, sifted
1–2 tablespoons fruit juice
1 teaspoon vanilla extract
several drops food coloring

1. Mix all ingredients together.

2. Paint icing on Gobble-Gobble Cakes using paint brushes.

BLESSINGS ARE THE GOOD things we have been given by God. Food, clothes, family, and friends are all blessings. A blessing can be many things—even a warm chocolate-chip cookie or a pretty flower! And a blessing isn't always something you can touch. A beautiful rainbow and a happy thought can both be blessings.

Here's a recipe that will give you a chance to think about your blessings. Your whole family can be a part of making this great ginger cake with lemon frosting. Use tube icing to draw a house shape on the top of the cake. Take turns having each person think of a blessing. As you name each blessing, put a gumdrop on the house. Try to remember not only the blessings that are *things,* but also the blessings that you can't touch, such as love and happiness. As you place each gumdrop on the cake, you may be surprised at how much you really have.

"Count Your Blessings" Ginger Cake

Things you'll need:

- 3 8-inch round cake pans
- large bowl
- measuring cups
- measuring spoons
- electric mixer
- 2 medium bowls
- spoon

Ingredients:

1 cup sugar
½ cup (1 stick) butter, softened
¼ cup shortening
3 eggs
1½ teaspoon vanilla extract

2 ½ cups all-purpose flour
1½ teaspoon baking soda
¾ teaspoon salt
1 teaspoon ginger
1 cup buttermilk

Teachable Moments

Children will naturally focus on material blessings, so remember to broaden the discussion by mentioning the kinds of things they might overlook. Include blessings such as a grand-mother's hug, a sister who shares, and happy memories.

1. Preheat the oven to 350 degrees.

2. Grease and flour three 8-inch round cake pans.

3. In a large bowl, cream sugar, butter, and shortening.

4. Add eggs, mixing well after each addition; add vanilla extract.

5. In a separate bowl, sift dry ingredients together then add to egg mixture alternately with buttermilk.

6. Beat on high speed for two minutes.

7. Pour batter into prepared pans and bake for 30 to 35 minutes, or until a wooden pick inserted in the center comes out clean.

8. Remove cake pans from the oven and cool.

Makes 1 three-layer cake.

Lemon Frosting

Ingredients:

½ cup (1 stick) butter, softened
4 ½ cups powdered sugar
1 teaspoon lemon extract
tube icing, any color
1–2 cups gumdrops

1. In a medium bowl, mix together butter and powdered sugar.

2. Stir in the lemon extract.

3. Spread frosting between cake layers and on top of cake. Draw a house shape on top of the cake with the tube icing. Decorate with gumdrops.

Frosts one three-layer cake.

17

It is important to count your blessings and to be thankful for them. One way of showing thankfulness for all you have is by giving some of what you have to others.

Giving

means presenting something to someone else or doing something for someone else—without expecting anything back from them. You can give many kinds of gifts to others. Some gifts may be presents, like toys and clothes. But gifts to others don't always have to be *things*. Some of the best kinds of gifts are gifts of time, hard work, and friendship. It may not always be easy to give, because giving takes away something from you. If giving can be hard and can take time, then why do it? There are two reasons. First, God tells us to give to others. Second, often you feel happier when you give someone a gift than when you receive a gift.

Christmas

 THERE IS ONE TIME each year when a special emphasis is placed on giving. This is the season of Christmas. Christmas is the Christian celebration of the birth of Jesus, God's Son. Because God gave this special gift, Christians remember and celebrate the birth of Jesus by giving gifts to others.

One of the many traditions celebrated at Christmas time is the Christmas tree. One legend says that on the night Jesus was born, the trees burst into full bloom! A tradition that came from Germany tells the story of Martin Luther, a German clergyman, finding a small fir tree in the woods on a starry night. Taking it home to his children at Christmas time, he decorated it with lighted candles to represent the stars.

During the Christmas season, a Christmas tree is often placed in the center of the house and decorated with lights and ornaments. To Christians, the tree is a symbol of the most important gift given by God, the gift of eternal life through Jesus. In celebration of this gift from God, family members and friends leave gifts to each other under the tree.

THIS YEAR AT CHRISTMAS time, make some pretty Christmas tree place-card holders for Christmas dinner. When you look at the Christmas tree, remember that it is both a beautiful part of the season and a reminder of the true meaning of Christmas.

Sugar Cone Christmas Trees

Things you'll need:

 wax paper

knife

measuring cup

construction paper

star-shaped pattern or cookie cutter

Ingredients:

5 sugar cones*
1 cup green icing*
assorted sprinkles
favorite small candies

1. Place sugar cones on wax paper.

2. Use a knife to cover each cone with green icing. Spread a generous amount on each cone so that peaks can be formed to look like a Christmas tree.

3. Place sprinkles and small candies on the wet icing tree to look like ornaments.

Teachable Moments

As the children make these place-card holders for Christmas dinner, discuss other Christmas symbols—stars, bells, wreaths, and angels. See if the children know or can determine what each of these might stand for in relation to the story of Jesus' birth. Stars symbolize the bright star that led the wise men to Jesus. Bells symbolize the church bells that ring to celebrate the birth of Jesus. Wreaths are circles of evergreen that symbolize the gift of eternal life. Angels symbolize the heavenly messages that announced the birth of Jesus.

4. Cut a star shape out of construction paper using a star-shaped pattern or cookie cutter. Write the name of each person attending your Christmas dinner on a star. Place the stars at the top of the Christmas trees.

5. After these trees are used as place-card holders to show everyone where to sit at the Christmas dinner, they can become part of your dessert!

Vary these amounts according to how many people will attend your Christmas dinner. This recipe makes 5 trees.

21

CHRISTMAS IS A TIME to receive gifts, but it also is a time to give gifts. Gifts you make yourself are especially appreciated. Making gifts takes time and work, and that shows the person receiving the gift that you really care!

Here's a sparkling gift recipe that you can make (with just a little help from Mom or Dad) to give to several friends this Christmas. The play-dough is non-edible, but it provides hours of fun. As a treat for all your hard work, we've included a yummy Christmas punch recipe just for you!

Play-dough Candy Canes
(A decoration gift—do not eat!)

Things you'll need:

- saucepan
- measuring cups
- measuring spoons
- wax paper

Ingredients:

1 cup all-purpose flour
½ cup salt
2 teaspoons cream of tartar
1 tablespoon cooking oil
1 cup water
several drops red food coloring
4 drops peppermint oil
2 tablespoons glitter

Teachable Moments

Let your child do as much of the work on this recipe as he can. Let him work hard, stirring and kneading the dough, because the more he puts into it, the more he will understand how hard work can make a gift more meaningful.

22

1. In a medium saucepan, mix dry ingredients. Add oil and water.

2. Divide mixture in half. Cook each half separately, adding red food coloring to one batch and leaving the other plain.

3. Cook the plain batch first and then the red, stirring constantly over low heat until mixture forms a ball in pan.

4. Remove from the pan and knead each batch separately, kneading two drops of peppermint oil and one-half tablespoon of glitter into each.

5. Place the two batches of play-dough on wax paper and divide each into four or five pieces. Roll into long strands. Twist one red and one white strand together to form a candy cane. Pinch ends together and bend into candy-cane shape. Sprinkle candy canes with remaining glitter.

Makes 4 or 5 small canes. For larger canes, make one full recipe for white dough and another for red dough.

23

Spicy Apple Punch

Things you'll need:

- large saucepan
- measuring cup
- Christmas mugs
- cinnamon stick (optional)

Ingredients:

1 gallon apple juice
½ cup red cinnamon candies

1. Pour apple juice into a large saucepan.

2. Stir in red cinnamon candies and heat over medium heat until thoroughly dissolved.

3. Serve with a cinnamon-stick stirrer, if you like.

Makes 8 8-ounce servings.

AT CHRISTMAS TIME, many stories are told of people who gave joyfully to others. One such tale is of a bishop named St. Nicholas. St. Nicholas was fascinated with the stories of the gifts brought to the baby Jesus, so he too gave children gifts at Christmas time, often secretly. He gave to others not because of what he might get back, but because he loved giving. Santa Claus, whose visits are eagerly awaited by American children each Christmas, is sometimes called St. Nicholas after this man.

Santa Claus is a wonderful example of the spirit of giving at Christmas time. Think of some people you could surprise with a gift at Christmas, and make these yummy Santa Bags to share with them—maybe a neighbor, a new friend, or your mail carrier. Give your gifts to them secretly, if you can, or just tell them that St. Nicholas himself asked you to pass them on!

Teachable Moments

As you make these Santa Bags with your child, emphasize the importance of giving without expecting anything in return. Help your child choose the people she will give to, knowing that, especially if she gives *secretly*, she will not receive anything in return.

Santa Bags

Things you'll need:

- medium bowl
- measuring cups
- measuring spoons
- small microwave-safe bowl
- cookie sheet
- pastry brush
- ribbon

Ingredients:

1 ½ cup Ricotta cheese
2 tablespoons strawberry preserves
1 tablespoon powdered sugar
1 6-ounce package chocolate morsels
1 egg, beaten
1 teaspoon vanilla extract
6 frozen phyllo sheets, thawed
¼ cup (½ stick) butter, melted
ribbon

1. Preheat oven to 375 degrees.

2. In a medium bowl, combine cheese, preserves, powdered sugar, chocolate morsels, egg, and vanilla extract.

3. In a small microwave-safe bowl, melt ¼ cup butter in a microwave oven.

4. Use a pastry brush to brush one phyllo sheet with butter.

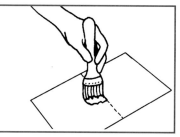

5. Fold the sheet in half side to side, brush again with butter, and fold in half lengthwise. Add the cheese mixture in the center of the folded phyllo sheet (3 tablespoons per bag).

6. Gather ends toward the center, completely enclosing the cheese mixture, and twist. Repeat with remaining phyllo and cheese.

7. Place bundles on a greased cookie sheet and bake for 17 minutes, or until browned.

8. Cool and wrap the twisted dough with a ribbon.

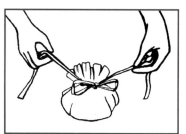

Makes 6 Santa Bags.

PART OF THE CHRISTMAS story is the story of wise men, also called kings or Magi. They traveled from the East, following a bright star, until they came to the place where Jesus was. With them the wise men brought valuable gifts of gold, incense, and myrrh.

Getting these gifts to Jesus had not been easy for the wise men. They had probably studied for many years just to be able to recognize this special star, and they traveled for a very long time to find Jesus. In fact, they probably didn't see the baby Jesus until many months or even years after He was born. Giving gifts to baby Jesus took hard work and sacrifice. The gifts the wise men brought were expensive, but it was their dedication to the search for God that was priceless.

It's important to remember during the Christmas season that giving isn't always easy. Think about the wise men as you make these "jeweled" Three Kings' Crowns. The recipe is difficult, but with hard work and a little help from Mom, you'll do a great job!

Teachable Moments

The focus of this activity is on sacrificial giving. One of the best ways a child can experience such giving is to give from money he has earned on his own. Arrange for your child to do odd jobs to earn money, and then let him buy a gift to give to a needy child through one of the giving programs offered in schools and churches at Christmas time.

Three Kings' Crowns

Things you'll need:

- 2 large non-metallic bowls
- measuring cups
- measuring spoons
- electric mixer
- clean kitchen towel
- cookie sheet

Ingredients:

2 packages active dry yeast
¾ cup warm water (110°)
2 cups lukewarm milk
¼ cup sugar
¼ cup (½ stick) butter, softened
1 tablespoon salt
7½ cups all-purpose flour
Royal Icing (see recipe, next page)
candied fruit

1. Mix the yeast and warm water in a large non-metallic bowl. Then stir in milk, sugar, butter, salt, and 3½ cups flour.

2. Stir thoroughly, adding enough of remaining 4 cups flour to keep dough from being too sticky.

3. Turn dough onto lightly floured surface; knead until smooth—about 12 minutes.

4. Spray a large non-metallic bowl with cooking spray and place the dough in the bowl. Turn once to coat.

5. Cover bowl with a clean kitchen towel and let dough rise in a warm place until doubled in size—about an hour.

6. Punch dough down and divide into quarters.

7. Take one quarter and pinch off one-third of it. This should be enough dough to roll into a cylinder one inch in diameter and five inches long. Bend the cylinder around to form a semi-circle and place on a cookie sheet that has been sprayed with cooking spray.

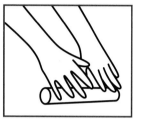 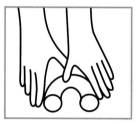

8. Take another quarter and divide it into four smaller cylinders each three inches long. Roll these tubes into a circle and position at the top of the crown.

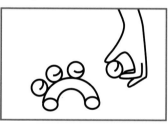

9. Repeat steps 7 and 8 for the remaining two crowns.

10. Place in a 425-degree oven and bake for 20 to 25 minutes. Remove and brush with frosting. Decorate with candied fruit.

Makes 3 crowns.

Royal Icing

Things you'll need:

- small bowl
- measuring cups
- measuring spoons
- spoon
- pastry brush

Ingredients:

2 cups powdered sugar
1 teaspoon vanilla extract
¼ cup milk

1. Mix ingredients together in a small bowl until smooth.

2. Brush over baked crowns until well glazed.

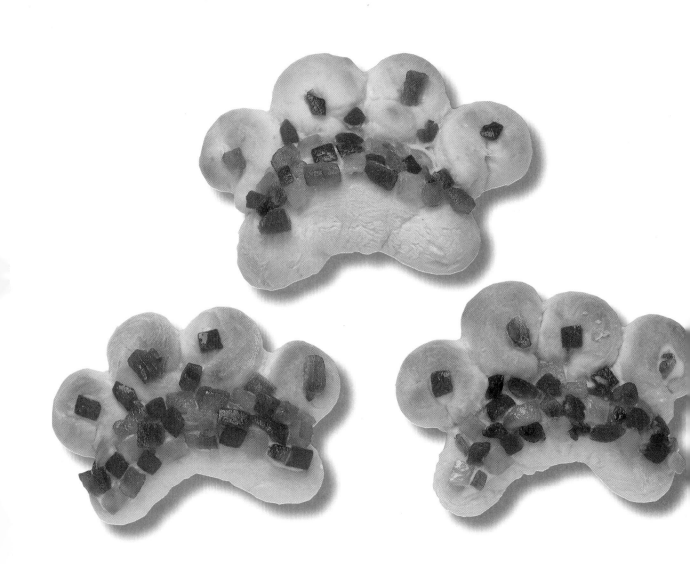

Love is a deep feeling of caring for another person. You love your parents, your grandparents, your brothers or sisters, and your friends. They love you, too.

Loving Others

Loving someone isn't always easy. Even though you love a person, he or she may make you sad or angry. For example, you may be really tired of your little sister getting into your things. But even though you are angry with her, you still love her. You may think the people you love already know you love them. But even if they do, it's important to say "I love you" because knowing that others love them makes people feel special. Saying "I love you" is only one of the many ways you can show people you care. Other ways include telling them something you like about them and being kind to them.

Valentine's Day

 VALENTINE'S DAY IS a special day in February when many people tell their friends and family how much they love them. They may give cards, candy, or flowers to the people they love.

You can make these yummy chocolate-dipped fish crackers with the funny "You're a Great Catch" message. Think of something special about each person you are giving a bag of fish to, and write that on the card. For example, "You're a Great Catch because you are fun to play with!"

Teachable Moments

Talk with your child about ways to show love to family and friends that don't involve gift-giving. Have her name different ways of treating people (for example, *helping, teasing, listening, arguing*). Decide whether each is loving or unloving.

"You're a Great Catch" Nibbles

Things you'll need:

- 2 medium microwave-safe bowls
- measuring cup
- measuring spoons
- spoon
- wax paper
- netting
- red and white construction paper
- marker
- ribbon

Ingredients:

1 bag fish-shaped pretzels
2 cups white chocolate morsels
red food coloring
2 tablespoons cream (optional)

1. Divide the fish-shaped pretzels into two groups (half a bag each).

2. Place 1 cup white chocolate morsels in each of two separate microwave-safe bowls and microwave each bowl at 40-second intervals on medium power, stirring between intervals. (For smoother consistency, add 1 tablespoon cream to each bowl of chocolate.)

3. Add red food coloring to one bowl to make chocolate red. Add a small amount of red coloring to other bowl to make pink, or leave as is for white.

4. Dip half the fish pretzels in the white (or pink) melted chocolate and lay out on wax paper. Dip the other half of the pretzels in the red chocolate and lay out on wax paper. Let pretzels dry completely.

5. To prepare gift, cut an 8-inch square of netting, lay flat, and spoon ½ cup of dry coated pretzels onto the net. Pull all the ends together, twist, and tie with a ribbon.

6. On a construction paper heart, write "You're a Great Catch because..." and fill in a special quality of your friend. Punch a hole in the heart and tie it on with the ribbon.

Makes 80 to 100 dipped fish pretzels.

Mother's Day

 MOMS ARE GREAT! Chances are, your mom has given you love and attention from the day you were born. And while she knows you love her, she loves to hear you say that you do.

Although you should show your mom you love her every day of the year, one special day has been set aside just to honor her—Mother's Day!

Here's a great recipe you can make for your mother on Mother's Day, or on any day you want to do something special for her. Get Dad or an older friend to help you make these Lemon Scones. You may want to make the dough the night before and leave it in the refrigerator to chill. In the morning, you'll be ready to make Mom a wonderful breakfast in bed! And don't forget the most important thing of all—to tell her how much you love her!

Teachable Moments

There are many ways you can help your children show their love for their mother. One great way is by helping the children make a coupon book. Coupons can be good for "one free room cleaning without complaining," "an undisturbed Saturday morning," or "a night out with friends, without coming home to a messy house!"

Flowery Lemon Scones

Things you'll need:

- large bowl
- measuring cups
- measuring spoons
- sifter
- fork
- spoon
- plastic wrap
- rolling pin
- rubber spatula
- cookie sheet
- flower-shaped cookie cutter

Ingredients:

2¼ cups all-purpose flour
1 teaspoon baking powder
¼ teaspoon baking soda
2 tablespoons sugar
½ cup (1 stick) butter, softened
½ cup cream
½ teaspoon lemon extract
½ teaspoon grated lemon rind

1. Preheat oven to 350 degrees.

2. Sift together flour, baking powder, baking soda, and sugar.

3. With a fork, cut in butter until mixture resembles corn meal.

4. Stir in cream, lemon extract, and grated lemon rind. Mix thoroughly to combine.

5. Shape dough into a ball. Wrap in plastic wrap and chill for several hours or overnight.

6. On a floured surface, roll out the dough to a ½-inch thickness. Cut scones with a flower-shaped cookie cutter.

7. Lightly spray cookie sheet with cooking spray. Place scones on the baking sheet and bake for 12 to 14 minutes, or until golden brown.

8. Serve scones with Mother's Day Tea.

Makes 2 dozen scones.

Mother's Day Tea

Things you'll need:

- tea cup
- measuring cup
- spoon
- measuring spoons
- kettle or pot for heating water

Ingredients:

1 cup cold water
1 tea bag
⅛ teaspoon almond extract
sugar to taste

1. Place tea bag in tea cup.

2. Bring water to a boil and pour over tea bag.

3. Let tea bag steep in hot water for three to five minutes (or until tea reaches strength your mom prefers).

4. Remove tea bag and stir in almond extract and sugar.

Makes 1 cup of tea.

Father's Day

DADS ARE SPECIAL, too—and they also have a special day.
Father's Day is a time to show love and appreciation to fathers.

Think about all your dad does for you. On Father's Day or any day you want
to honor your dad, make a card that tells Dad how you feel about him.
Write a sentence like "My favorite thing to do with Daddy is..."or "My Dad is
great because..."—and then finish the sentence. Here's a great recipe that
Dad is sure to love. And don't forget the most important part of the day—a
great big hug, a kiss, and an "I love you, Daddy!"

Teachable Moments

While you prepare Dad's
Cheesecake, talk about respect.
Explain that showing respect for
a father is one of the greatest
ways you can show him you love
him. Give specific ideas on how
to show respect for a parent—
obeying the first time you're told,
coming when called, and
looking at him when you're
talking with him.

Dad's Cheesecake

Things you'll need:

- medium bowl
- large bowl
- small bowl
- measuring cups
- measuring spoons
- 8" spring-form pan
- spoon
- electric mixer
- heart-shaped cookie cutter

Ingredients:

- 1 cup all-purpose flour
- ½ cup (1 stick) butter, softened
- ¼ cup powdered sugar
- 2 8-ounce packages cream cheese, softened
- 2 eggs
- ⅔ cup sugar
- 1 teaspoon vanilla extract
- 1 cup sour cream
- 2 tablespoons sugar
- 1 teaspoon vanilla extract
- cherry pie filling

1. Preheat oven to 400 degrees.

2. In a medium bowl, mix the first three ingredients together with clean hands to form a soft dough.

3. Press the dough firmly and evenly against the bottom and sides of an 8-inch spring-form pan.

4. Bake for 12 to 15 minutes, or until light brown. Cool. Reduce oven temperature to 375 degrees.

5. In a large bowl, cream the cheese and stir in eggs, ⅔ cup sugar, and one teaspoon vanilla extract. Beat until well blended.

6. Pour cheese mixture into crust and bake in 375-degree oven for 20 minutes.

7. Remove from oven and let stand for 15 minutes. Increase oven temperature to 425 degrees.

8. In a small bowl, combine sour cream, remaining sugar, and remaining vanilla extract. Spread over the top of the cheesecake.

9. Return to a 425-degree oven for ten minutes. Cool, then chill in refrigerator.

10. When cooled, remove the spring-form ring, transfer cake onto serving plate, and place a large heart-shaped cookie cutter in the center of the cake to make a heart-shaped impression. Fill in with cherries from cherry pie filling to make a heart.

Makes 1 large cheesecake.

Grandparents' Day

 ARE THERE SOME people in your family who love you so much that it's silly? Maybe there are some who can never get enough hugs and kisses. They have a little more time, and they seem to be a little more patient with you than your parents are. They don't always care if you have a cookie before dinner, forget to brush your teeth, or stay up late. In fact, if you asked them to get you the moon from the sky, they would probably say "Okay, Honey!" These wonderful people are probably your grandparents.

Did you know there is a special day set aside in September to remember your grandparents? This Grandparents' Day, let your grandparents know how special you think they are. If they live far away, make a pretty card to send in the mail. If they live near you, invite them over for a special Sunday dinner. Make these pretty fruit parfaits and a card that expresses your love.

Teachable Moments

Whether or not your family celebrates Grandparents' Day each year, have your child begin a tradition of calling, writing, or doing something special for a grandparent on a certain day each month. This could become a tradition that your child continues for years.

Grandparents' Parfaits

Ingredients:

2 cups strawberries, chopped
2 cups kiwi, chopped
other assorted fruits, chopped
1 cup whipping cream, whipped

1. In a small bowl, mix together the chopped fruits.

2. Place two tablespoons of the fruit in the bottom of each parfait glass.

3. Top with two tablespoons whipped cream. Repeat this process until each parfait cup is filled.

4. Place a dollop of whipped cream on the top of each parfait and top with your favorite piece of fruit.

Serves four. Increase fruit and cream as needed to serve more people.

As long as people have lived, they have searched for meaning in their lives and have tried to understand their Creator. Faith is belief and trust in God. Worship is how people show love and respect for God.

Respect for God

Many of the holidays we celebrate are religious holidays. They are times when we give special attention to the traditions of our faith and show respect for God.  Learning more about the religious holidays you celebrate with your family will make these holidays more meaningful. And learning about the religious celebrations of other faiths is good, too, because it will help you understand other people's beliefs and respect them, even if you believe differently.

Easter

 EASTER SUNDAY IS a joyous Christian celebration. Christians believe that because Jesus was crucified and rose from the dead, all who believe in Him will live forever after they die. For that reason, Easter is a celebration of new life and new hope.

Special church services are held on Easter Sunday to remember Jesus' resurrection from death, and many people wear new clothes as a celebration of spiritual new life. Families gather together after services for special dinners. Children often hunt Easter eggs, which are another Easter symbol. Just as the egg holds new life, so the Christian believes new spiritual life is found in following Jesus Christ.

Make these Easter Basket Cookies and fill a spring basket with flower-, chick-, and egg-shaped cookies. This basket could be the centerpiece for your dinner table or a gift to someone you love.

Teachable Moments

As your child paints the Easter cookies, emphasize the concept of new life and new birth. To explain this concept further, give your child a hard-boiled egg. Have him pretend that the shell is a bad habit, or something he needs to change about himself. Have him peel the egg (peeling away the old habit) to reveal a fresh, new self inside.

Easter Basket Cookies

Things you'll need:

- large bowl
- medium bowl
- measuring cups
- measuring spoons
- electric mixer
- sifter
- plastic wrap
- rolling pin
- Easter cookie cutters (eggs, chicks, flowers, etc.)
- cookie sheet
- spatula

Ingredients:

1 cup (2 sticks) butter, softened
2 cups sugar
2 eggs
2 teaspoons vanilla extract
4 cups all-purpose flour, sifted
2 teaspoons baking powder
½ teaspoon salt

1. Preheat oven to 375 degrees.

2. In a large bowl, cream butter and sugar thoroughly.

3. Add eggs, mixing well after each; add vanilla extract.

4. In a separate bowl, sift together flour, baking powder, and salt; add to egg mixture.

5. Shape dough into a ball, wrap in plastic wrap, and refrigerate for one hour.

6. Dust a cutting surface with flour and sugar. (Adding sugar will help keep the cookies from becoming overly dry.)

7. Place dough on prepared board and roll to ¼-inch thickness.

8. With cookie cutters, cut Easter shapes and lift with spatula to place on a cookie sheet.

9. Bake for 10 or 12 minutes, or until lightly browned. Cool before painting.

Makes 2 dozen cookies.

Colored Whipping Cream

Things you'll need:

4 small bowls

measuring cup

small clean paint brushes

Ingredients:

1 pint whipping cream
assorted food coloring
sprinkles or decorations (optional)
tube icing (optional)

1. Evenly distribute the whipping cream into each of four separate bowls.

2. Add different food colorings to the bowls until you get the colors you want.

3. Using a small clean paint brush, dip into the dyed cream and paint cookies.

4. If desired, add sprinkles or other edible decorations or outline with tube icing.

Lent

LENT, OR "HOLY SPRING," is the forty days before Easter when members of many Christian groups prepare for the coming of Easter. Lent is a time when people do without certain things they enjoy, especially foods, so they might be reminded of the importance of the Lenten season—Jesus' sacrifice. It is a time to focus on God's love for us.

One symbol that represents the prayerful season of Lent is the pretzel. Pretzels were probably first made by monks using the unleavened dough of Lent. The twists in the pretzel are said to represent hands crossed in prayer. Some say that monks would make pretzels and feed them to children as they taught about prayer.

Teachable Moments

This would be a good opportunity to talk to your child about prayer. Discuss the times when your family prays—mealtimes, bedtime, etc. Talk about how prayer to God can take place at any time and in any location.

44

"Praying Hands" Pretzels

Things you'll need:

- 2 large non-metallic bowls
- measuring cups
- measuring spoons
- spoon
- cookie sheet

Ingredients:

1 cup warm water (110°)
1 package active dry yeast
2¾ cups all-purpose flour, sifted
   and divided
2 tablespoons butter, softened
½ teaspoon salt
1 tablespoon sugar
coarse salt

1. Combine the warm water and yeast in a large non-metallic bowl. Dissolve and stir for about four minutes.

2. Add 1½ cups flour, butter, salt, and sugar. Stir thoroughly to combine.

3. Stir in remaining flour and knead until the dough loses its stickiness, about 15 times.

4. Place dough in a large greased non-metallic bowl and cover. Let sit until it doubles in size, about 1½ hours.

5. Punch down and divide into 12 pieces. Roll the pretzel pieces into "ropes" about 17 inches long. Pull up both ends and tuck under to form the pretzel shape, as shown.

6. Place pretzels on a greased cookie sheet and let double in size, about an hour. Sprinkle with coarse salt.

7. Bake in a 350-degree oven for 12 to 14 minutes or until browned.

Makes 12 pretzels.

Passover

 PASSOVER IS AN eight-day festival celebrated by Jewish people each spring. It remembers the time when the Israelites escaped from slavery in Egypt. The story of the first Passover is told in the book of Exodus in the Bible.

Matzo, or unleavened bread, is eaten by Jewish (or Israelite) people during Passover. When the Israelites left Egypt, they had very little time to prepare for their journey. Following God's instructions, they quickly made an unleavened dough (matzo meal) to take with them in order that they could make bread on their journey. You can read about this in Exodus 12:33–34.

In today's Passover celebrations, Jewish families gather together for a special meal called a Seder. The ancient story of Passover is told during the Seder. During the dinner, a special matzo called the *afikomen* is hidden. The children make a game of searching for the *afikomen* at the conclusion of the Seder, and whoever finds it gets a reward. Then everyone eats a piece of the *afikomen* for blessings in the coming year.

Here's an interesting recipe that uses matzos, which are so important during Passover time.

Teachable Moments

As you make this recipe with your child, talk about Passover and the story behind the unleavened bread. Because Passover is a celebration of freedom, talk with her about the need that all people have to be free. The Israelites were willing to leave their homes and march into the desert in order to be free to worship God.

Cinnamon Matzo Toast

Things you'll need:

- colander
- large bowl
- measuring cups
- measuring spoons
- electric mixer
- skillet
- spatula
- sifter

Ingredients:

4 pieces matzo bread
4 cups boiling water
2 eggs
¼ cup milk
½ teaspoon salt
1½ teaspoon cinnamon
2 tablespoons butter
1 cup powdered sugar

1. Break the matzos in half. Arrange them in a colander.

2. Pour boiling water over the matzos and drain quickly.

3. In a large bowl, beat the eggs with the milk and add the salt and ½ teaspoon cinnamon.

4. Soak the matzos in the egg mixture for one minute on each side.

5. Melt the butter in a skillet. Place the matzos in the skillet over medium heat and fry until golden brown on each side, turning with a spatula.

6. Combine powdered sugar with 1 teaspoon cinnamon; stir thoroughly. Sift this mixture over the hot matzos.

Makes 8 pieces of toast.

Sunday

 EVERY WEEK, SUNDAY is a day that many people set aside for special purposes. According to Genesis, the first book in the Bible, God made the earth in six days, and on the seventh day He rested. Because God rested on the seventh day, the people of Israel called the seventh day the Sabbath. They rested and worshiped God on that day.

For most Christians, the first day of the week is a special day of worship and rest from the week's work. Many Christian families spend Sunday morning in worship and Sunday afternoon resting and enjoying family activities. Here's a fun Sunday morning breakfast recipe idea your family can enjoy together.

Teachable Moments

Talk about the value of Sunday as a day of worship, family time, and rest. Stress the importance of doing homework and chores on Saturday, so that Sunday can be a special day your family can enjoy and look back upon with fond memories.

Sunny Sunday Animal Pancakes

Things you'll need:

- medium bowl
- measuring cups
- measuring spoons
- electric mixer
- skillet
- rubber spatula
- wax paper
- animal-shaped cookie cutters

Ingredients:

1 egg
¾ cup milk
2 tablespoons vegetable oil
1 cup all-purpose flour
2 tablespoons sugar
3 teaspoons baking powder
½ teaspoon salt
1 teaspoon vanilla extract
raisins and strawberries for
    faces
syrup

1. In a medium mixing bowl, beat egg thoroughly. Add remaining ingredients and mix until smooth.

2. Spray a skillet with cooking spray and heat over medium heat. When skillet is ready, pour three tablespoons batter onto the skillet for each pancake.

3. Cook pancakes over medium heat until they are browned around the edges. Turn and cook on the other side until golden brown.

4. Remove from pan with spatula and place on wax paper. Cut each pancake with a favorite animal cookie cutter.

5. Top with raisins and strawberries to make faces.

6. Serve with your favorite syrup.

Makes 6 to 8 pancakes.

49

Showing courage means facing something difficult, painful, or even dangerous. Fire fighters are courageous when they risk their lives to save people or nature. Police officers show courage when they risk danger to keep people safe.

Courage

But you don't have to fight fires or chase criminals to show courage. All kinds of people show courage. Children who have a disease that makes life difficult or painful show courage every day that they fight to stay healthy. People who have physical or mental challenges that make everyday life harder for them than it is for others must be courageous, too. Courage is also standing up for what you believe in and what you think is right. Some people may make fun of you when you stand up for what you believe in, so that takes courage. Sometimes you may stand alone. Many of the holidays we celebrate remind us of the courage of people who lived before us. Because of their courage, our lives and our world are better.

Teachable Moments

Talk with your child about people you know who are courageous. Explain that she may face situations in which she will have to show courage. For example, she may get lost in the grocery store, or someone may try to sell her drugs when she is older.

Columbus Day

 IN 1492, A MAN named Christopher Columbus showed courage. At that time, most people thought the world was flat. They believed that if you sailed to the end of it, you would fall off! Columbus believed that the world was round. Even though people laughed at his opinion, he decided to find the truth. He gathered a crew, asked the King and Queen of Spain to give him the money he would need, and sailed west. Columbus didn't know if his crew would have enough food and water, because he didn't know how long the journey would take. He couldn't be sure he would ever reach land. But he sailed bravely on and found the land we now call America!

As you celebrate Columbus Day, make these delicious Pita Pocket Ships sandwiches, and remember the courage of Christopher Columbus!

Pita Pocket Ships

Things you'll need:

knife
cutting board
measuring cup
measuring spoons
medium bowl
spoon
wooden picks

Ingredients:

2 chicken breasts, cooked and
  cubed
1 piece bacon, cooked and
  crumbled
1 small Granny Smith apple, peeled,
  cored, and cubed

¼ cup mayonnaise
½ teaspoon salt
¼ teaspoon black pepper
4 pita bread halves
shredded lettuce
4 celery stalks
2 pieces American cheese, halved
  diagonally

1. Combine the chicken, bacon, apple, mayonnaise, salt, and pepper in a medium bowl to make chicken salad.

2. Spoon chicken salad into each pita bread half.

3. Top with shredded lettuce.

4. Stick a celery stalk in the middle of each pita sandwich. With a wooden pick, pin half a slice of cheese to each celery stalk to resemble a sail.

Makes 4 pita sandwiches.

Martin Luther King, Jr.'s, Birthday

 MARTIN LUTHER KING, JR., was a courageous man who spent most of his life trying to get people of different races to live together peacefully. Dr. King traveled around the country teaching that the color of a person's skin was not as important as "the content of his character." His famous "I have a dream" speech expressed his hope that someday all people, regardless of color, would live happily together.

Dr. King didn't live long enough to see his dream come true. Many people were afraid of his ideas, and one of those people killed him. But Dr. King's dream has lived on, and in January we celebrate this courageous man's birthday.

Dr. King dreamed of a better world. You, too, can follow such a dream. Make these Dream Cakes and think about what your dream for a better world would be. Think very hard—it may be a dream that you keep forever!

Teachable Moments

Help your child name some things in the world that need improvement, and then help him think of specific ways to work on these problems. For example, if the problem is that people are too selfish, he can help by sharing with others. If the problem is pollution, he can help by not being a polluter himself.

Dream Cakes

Things you'll need:

- large bowl
- measuring cup
- measuring spoons
- electric mixer
- 12-hole muffin pan
- paper muffin liners
- serrated knife
- medium bowl
- rubber spatula

Ingredients:

1 box angel food cake mix
2 cups whipping cream
½ teaspoon peppermint extract
1 teaspoon red food coloring
3 tablespoons powdered sugar

1. Preheat oven to 350 degrees.

2. Prepare the angel food cake batter in a large bowl according to package directions.

3. Line a muffin pan with 12 paper muffin liners. Spoon batter into papers, filling each ¾ full.

4. Bake cupcakes for 15 to 20 minutes, or until lightly browned.

5. Remove cupcakes from pan and cool.

6. Remove paper liners. Cut each cupcake in half horizontally, using a serrated knife.

7. In a medium bowl, whip the whipping cream with the peppermint extract, food coloring, and powdered sugar.

8. Using the spatula, spread the top of the bottom half of each cupcake with the colored whipped cream. Place the top half of each cupcake on the cream-topped bottom half and freeze until firm. Refrigerate remaining whipped cream.

9. Cover tops of frozen cupcakes with remaining whipped cream and freeze until ready to serve.

Makes 12 cupcakes.

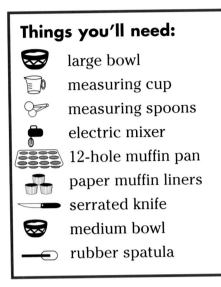

El Cinco de Mayo

 CINCO DE MAYO means "fifth of May." It is a Mexican holiday that celebrates the Mexican army's brave defense of their country when the French army tried to take over Mexico. About 2,000 Mexican soldiers defeated almost 6,000 French soldiers, saving the nation. The date of this courageous battle is now celebrated as Mexican Independence Day.

Many wonderful things have come to our country from Mexico. Just think — if the brave Mexican soldiers had not won that battle, we might not have piñatas, tortillas, or chocolate!

This year, celebrate *Cinco de Mayo* with Mexican Hot Chocolate and a loaf of French bread, and remember the courage of the Mexican soldiers so many years ago.

Teachable Moments

Because this activity focuses on the courage of people in the past, discuss stories of courage from your own family history, like a grandfather's courage in World War II. Remind your child of times when she has shown courage—standing up for a friend or helping a younger child. Your courage is like a muscle—each time you exercise it, it gets stronger!

Mexican Hot Chocolate

Things you'll need:

- saucepan
- measuring cups
- measuring spoons
- spoon
- portable electric mixer or rotary beater
- mugs

Ingredients:

⅓ cup sugar
⅓ cup cocoa
¼ teaspoon salt
½ teaspoon cinnamon
1½ cup half-and-half
4½ cups milk
cinnamon sticks

1. Mix the sugar, cocoa, salt, and cinnamon in a saucepan.

2. Add half-and-half and milk. Stir and heat thoroughly over low heat.

3. With a portable electric mixer or rotary beater, whip hot chocolate until foamy.

4. Pour into mugs and serve with a cinnamon stick stirrer. Enjoy with slices of French bread.

Makes 4 to 6 servings.

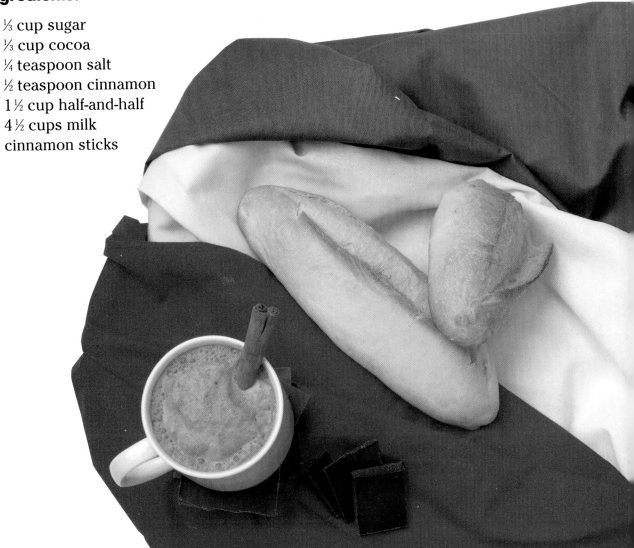

Memorial Day

 SHOWING COURAGE ISN'T easy. When you read about courageous people, you learn that many of them gave up their lives defending their beliefs or their country.

On Memorial Day, we remember Americans who died in wars while serving our country and supporting freedom. Memorial Day is celebrated with parades and speeches. It is a day for thinking about our freedom and honoring those who courageously fought and died for that freedom.

Teachable Moments

Cut strips of red, white, and blue construction paper. Have your child use a glue stick to join these in a long chain. Explain that, even if you used an entire package of construction paper and had a chain that wrapped around your whole house, you still wouldn't have as many links as there are people who have died defending our country and the freedom it stands for.

Red, White, and Blue Courage Cakes

Things you'll need:

- large bowl
- measuring cups
- measuring spoons
- electric mixer
- 3 medium bowls
- spoons
- jelly-roll pan
- wax paper
- knife or wooden skewer
- wooden pick
- cooling rack
- star-shaped cookie cutters

Ingredients:

1 box white cake mix
red food coloring
blue food coloring
white canned frosting,
   optional
red cinnamon candies
   or sprinkles

1. Preheat oven to 350 degrees.

2. Prepare the cake mix according to the package directions.

3. Divide the batter in thirds and place in three separate bowls. To one bowl add one to two teaspoons red food coloring (depending on desired color) and mix well. Add blue food coloring to the batter in the second bowl, and leave the batter in the third bowl white.

4. Line the jelly-roll pan with wax paper. Spoon the three batters into the pan in a checkerboard fashion. Swirl with a knife or wooden skewer.

5. Bake for 15 to 20 minutes, or until wooden pick inserted into the middle comes out clean. Remove from oven and cool on a cooling rack.

6. Cut the cooled cake with star-shaped cookie cutters.

7. Leave cakes plain or ice cakes with white canned frosting. Top with red cinnamon candies or sprinkles.

Makes 25 to 30 cakes.

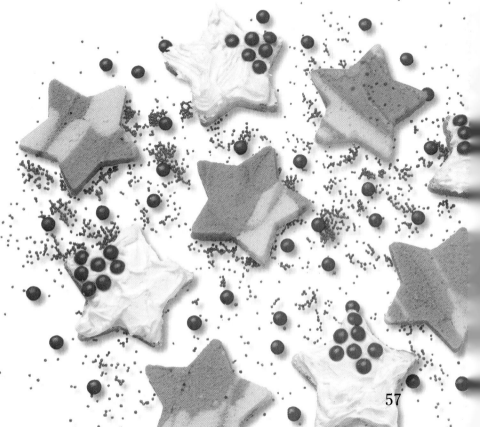

Everything that has been handed down to you from the people who lived before you is a part of your heritage. Your heritage includes things you can't touch, such as your family name. It also includes things you can touch, such as a great-grandfather's watch or a grandmother's piano. Some of the foods you eat may be part of your heritage, such as Aunt Mary's peanut brittle or Dad's barbecued chicken.

Enjoying Your Heritage

Many of the holidays you celebrate are part of your heritage, too, because they have been handed down from people who lived before you. One reason these have been handed down is simply that they are fun! And no matter how busy you might get with learning and growing, sometimes it's nice just to be with friends and have a good time.

St. Patrick's Day

ST. PATRICK'S DAY is the "green" holiday celebrated by the people of Ireland and Irish-Americans. When it first started, it was a holy day

Teachable Moments

The point of this activity is to have fun celebrating St. Patrick's Day. Why not serve an all green breakfast? Have the biscuit dough already made, and let children form their own "snakes." Serve with green butter shamrocks and green scrambled eggs—and don't forget a secret "pot of gold" (gold foil-wrapped chocolate coins) hidden somewhere in the house!

honoring St. Patrick, a Christian missionary to Ireland. Legend says that St. Patrick was a preacher who used the shamrock (a three-leaf clover) to illustrate the Trinity— God, Jesus, and the Holy Spirit. Another legend says St. Patrick drove all the snakes in Ireland to the seashore, where they drowned!

St. Patrick's Day is now celebrated on March 17. Many people celebrate by wearing green clothes and shamrocks. People also watch out for sneaky little leprechauns, because, as the legend goes, if someone catches one of these little green people, the leprechaun must take that person to a pot of gold!

St. Patrick's Day Snake Biscuits

Things you'll need:

- large bowl
- measuring cups
- measuring spoons
- fork
- small bowl
- spoon
- rolling pin
- knife
- cookie sheet

Ingredients:

⅓ cup shortening
2 cups all-purpose flour or cake flour
2 teaspoons baking powder
¼ teaspoon baking soda
¼ teaspoon salt
⅛ teaspoon black pepper
¾ cup buttermilk
2 teaspoons green food coloring

1. Preheat oven to 350 degrees.

2. In a large bowl, mix together the flour, baking powder, baking soda, salt, and pepper. Using a fork, mix in the shortening until mixture resembles coarse crumbs.

3. In a small bowl, stir together the buttermilk and food coloring.

4. Add the liquid mixture to the flour mixture and stir until dough forms a ball.

5. Place dough on a lightly floured surface and knead 12 times.

6. Roll dough into a square 8 to 10 inches across and cut into ½-inch strips. Place strips on cookie sheet and curve the dough to resemble a snake.

7. Bake for 10 to 12 minutes, or until lightly browned.

Makes about 8 to 10 biscuits.

Green Shamrock Butter

Things you'll need:

- small bowl
- electric mixer
- measuring cup
- spoon
- wax paper
- knife
- shamrock-shaped cookie cutter

Ingredients:

½ cup (1 stick) butter, softened

several drops green food coloring

1. In a small bowl, beat the butter until very smooth.

2. Add the green food coloring and continue to beat until thoroughly combined.

3. Scoop out onto wax paper and roll to form a cylinder about an inch in diameter. Place in refrigerator to harden.

4. When hardened, slice the butter into ¼-inch slices and cut with shamrock cookie cutter. Refrigerate until ready to serve.

Makes 20 or more pats.

Halloween

MANY AMERICAN CHILDREN look forward to Halloween each fall. While lots of families prefer not to celebrate the scary side of this event—witches, ghosts, and spiders—it can be fun to have a costume party.

This Halloween, why not have a circus party? Send out tiger invitations to your friends and have everyone dress as a favorite circus character. Play lots of games and serve popcorn and peanuts. And here's a fun recipe for Tiger Tail Twists cookies to make ahead of time or at the party. Make Halloween a time for fun and surprises rather than a time for being afraid!

Follow the tiger's trail to a circus party!

Where _____

When _____

Dress as your favorite circus animal

Teachable Moments

Many parents would rather not celebrate Halloween at all, but for children it's a favorite holiday. Use the occasion for dressing in fun costumes and gathering with friends or neighbors. Coordinating a "Fall Festival" may be a healthier approach than ignoring Halloween altogether.

Tiger Tail Twists

Things you'll need:

- 2 medium bowls
- measuring cups
- measuring spoons
- grater
- electric mixer
- small bowl
- spoons
- knife
- wax paper
- cookie sheet

Chocolate Sugar Cookie Dough

Ingredients:

1½ cup powdered sugar
1¼ cup butter, softened
1 egg
3 cups all-purpose flour
½ cup cocoa
¼ teaspoon salt

1. In a medium bowl, mix sugar, butter, and egg.

2. Mix in flour, cocoa, and salt; stir until dough forms a ball.

3. Place dough on a piece of wax paper and roll to form a one-inch cylinder.

4. Refrigerate for one hour.

Orange Sugar Cookie Dough

Ingredients:

1½ cup powdered sugar
1 cup (2 sticks) butter, softened
1 egg
1 teaspoon vanilla extract
2 teaspoons fresh grated orange rind
¼ teaspoon salt
2 teaspoons orange food coloring
2½ cups all-purpose flour
1 teaspoon baking soda

1. In a medium bowl, mix sugar, butter, egg, vanilla extract, orange rind, salt, and food coloring.

2. In a separate bowl, stir together flour and baking soda, then add to egg mixture; stir until dough forms a ball.

3. Place dough on a piece of wax paper and roll to form a one-inch cylinder.

4. Refrigerate for one hour.

Tiger Tails

1. Preheat oven to 350 degrees.

2. Cut ½-inch slices from the chocolate and orange doughs. Roll each piece in hands to form a tail-like rope about five inches long.

3. Twist one chocolate and one orange rope of dough together to form a "tail." Pinch ends together and curl one end around.

4. Place tiger tails on a lightly greased cookie sheet and bake for eight to ten minutes.

Makes 2 dozen tiger tails.

(As a variation, try making paw prints.)

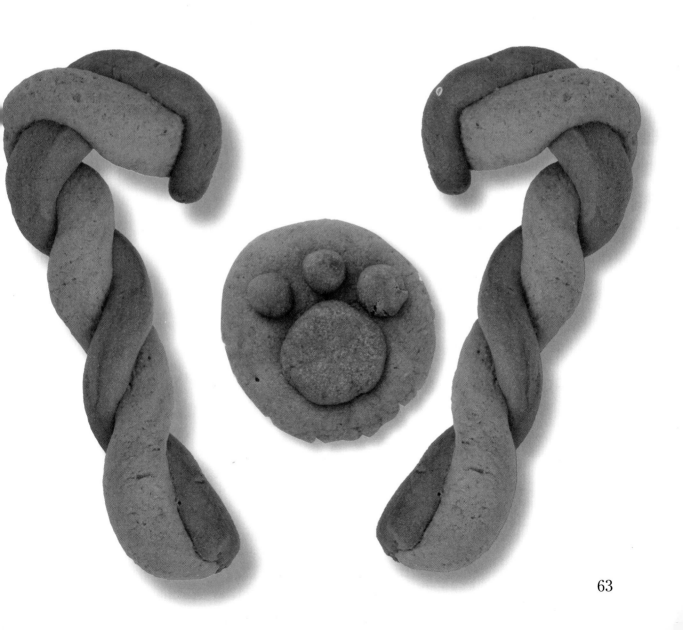

Purim

 PURIM IS A JOYFUL HOLIDAY for the Jewish people. It is a celebration of the time when a brave young queen saved great numbers of her Jewish kinspeople from being killed by the Persians. The story is told in the book of Esther in the Bible.

Esther was a Jewish woman who married the king of Persia. The prime minister of Persia was an evil man named Haman. Haman hated the Jews, so he tried to trick the king into killing all of them. Esther found out about the trick and bravely went before the king, risking her life to save her people. When the king heard of the plan, he had evil Haman killed and saved the Jews' lives.

Jewish children often dress up in costumes and act out the story of Esther at Purim parties. *Hamantaschen* (Hah-mehn-TAH-shen), three-cornered cakes, are served on Purim. These are also called Haman's Hats, because the jailers who took Haman away were said to have worn three-cornered hats.

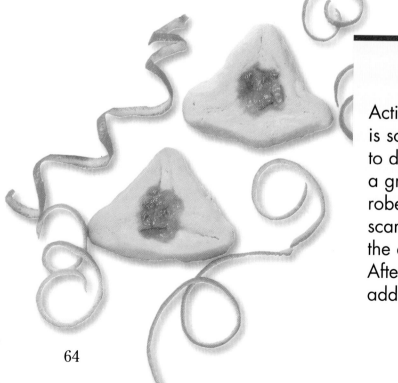

Teachable Moments

Acting out a favorite Bible story is something many children love to do, and the story of Esther is a great one to dramatize. Use robes for costumes and towels or scarves for headdresses to make the drama more enjoyable. Afterward, the Haman's Hats will add another touch of festivity.

Haman's Hats

Things you'll need:

- 2 medium bowls
- measuring cups
- measuring spoons
- electric mixer
- plastic wrap
- knife
- cookie sheet

Ingredients:

½ cup shortening
¼ cup oil
¾ cup sugar
½ cup orange juice
2 teaspoons vanilla
  extract
3 cups all-purpose flour
2 teaspoons baking
  powder
pinch of salt
½ cup orange
  marmalade

1. Preheat oven to 350 degrees.

2. Cream shortening, oil, sugar, orange juice, and vanilla extract in a medium bowl.

3. In a separate bowl, stir together flour, baking powder, and salt, then add shortening mixture; stir thoroughly to combine.

4. Form dough into two-inch cylinders and wrap with plastic wrap. Refrigerate until firm.

5. Cut ⅜- inch slices from the chilled dough and place on a cookie sheet. Pinch the round piece of dough on the top and sides to form a triangle shape.

6. Place ½ teaspoon orange marmalade in the center of the triangle.

7. Bake for 15 minutes, or until the edges are lightly browned.

Makes 2 ½ dozen pastries.

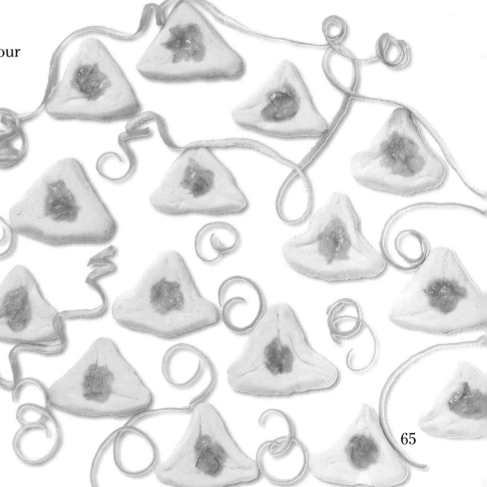

65

Birthdays!

 ONE SPECIAL DAY each year is set aside just for you—your birthday!

You are a unique, one-of-a-kind person. You were given a special name when you were born, a name you will always have as a part of your heritage. You have your own special looks, feelings, and fingerprints that don't match any other person's in the whole world!

Celebrate on your birthday! Think about how special God made you, and say a thank-you prayer.

Teachable Moments

You don't have to rent three clowns and a juggler to make your child's birthday a special day. A birthday celebration with just your family can be a wonderful opportunity to show your child how important he is to you. Let him participate in preparing his own birthday meal. During the meal, have each family member tell one thing he or she appreciates about the birthday child.

Birthday Present Sandwich

Things you'll need:

- measuring cups
- measuring spoons
- knife
- cutting board
- wooden picks

Ingredients:

2 pieces white bread
2 pieces pumpernickel bread
1 cup ham, finely chopped
1 tablespoon sweet pickle relish
¼ cup mayonnaise
3 green onion tops cut into strips

1. Stack the pieces of bread on a cutting board and cut the crust from the bread.

2. Spread one side of three pieces of bread with the ham mixture.

3. Stack the slices so the spread is inside.

4. Wrap two green onion strips around the sandwich and secure with a wooden pick to resemble the ribbons on a package.

5. Cut one green onion strip smaller and fray the edges with a knife. Secure in the middle with a wooden pick.

Makes 1 sandwich.

Pepper and Cheese Hearts

Things you'll need:

- knife
- cutting board
- small heart-shaped cookie cutter

Ingredients:

1 large bell pepper
2 to 3 American cheese slices

1. Cut and seed a bell pepper. Cut in halves or fourths lengthwise to make a side that can be laid flat on the cutting board.

2. Cut heart shapes out of green pepper with a small heart-shaped cookie cutter.

3. Remove plastic from cheese and cut heart shapes out of cheese.

4. Serve pepper and cheese hearts as appetizers or with your birthday meal.

Makes 4 to 6 cheese hearts and 2 to 3 pepper hearts.

New Year's Day

 NEW YEAR'S DAY is the first day of January—the very first day of each new year. New Year's Day is a day for new beginnings. It is a day when many people make resolutions to do good or to do better in the coming year. You might make a resolution to get along better with your brother or sister, or to try harder to keep your room clean.

Some people celebrate the new year by staying up until midnight on New Year's Eve and making noise and singing as the new year comes in. Many Americans spend New Year's Day watching football games on television and eating black-eyed peas. Black-eyed peas are said to bring riches in the new year!

This New Year's Day, make your own resolutions to do better in the coming year. And don't forget to eat some black-eyed peas along with these Ham and Cheese Mini-Muffins.

Teachable Moments

Try making some resolutions as a family this year. Over black-eyed peas and corn muffins, talk about some bad habits your family could change. For each bad habit you give up, substitute a good one!

Savory Black-eyed Peas

Things you'll need:

- colander
- measuring cups
- measuring spoons
- large saucepan
- spoon

Ingredients:

1 cup dried black-eyed peas
1 piece bacon
3½ cups water
½ teaspoon salt
¼ teaspoon black pepper

1. Rinse peas thoroughly in a colander.

2. Fry one piece bacon in saucepan until crisp. Drain and crumble into pan.

3. Add peas and water to saucepan and heat to boiling. Boil two minutes; remove from heat. Cover and let stand one hour. Stir.

4. Add salt and pepper; add more water if needed.

5. Place pan on stove and return to boiling. Reduce heat, cover, and let simmer for 1½ hours or until the peas are tender.

Makes 4 servings.

Ham and Cheese Mini-Muffins

Things you'll need:

- bowl
- electric mixer
- measuring cup
- knife
- cutting board
- mini-muffin pan
- paper muffin liners
- spoon

Ingredients:

1 box cornbread muffin mix
⅓ cup ham, finely diced
⅓ cup cheese, shredded

1. Preheat oven to 350 degrees.

2. Prepare cornbread muffin batter according to the package directions.

3. Stir in the diced ham and cheese.

4. Line a mini-muffin pan with paper muffin liners. Spoon batter into papers, filling each ¾ full.

5. Bake for 15 minutes, or until muffins are golden brown.

Makes 2 dozen muffins.

Yesterday is now in the past. So is last week, last year, and your last birthday. All of these are times that have gone by.

Respect for the Past

If something is in the past, then why think about it any more? There is a very good reason. Learning about the past can help us understand problems we have today. We can learn to be better people by hearing about both the mistakes people made in the past and the good things they did.

Presidents' Day

PRESIDENTS' DAY is the third Monday in February. On this day we honor two very important presidents from our nation's past— George Washington and Abraham Lincoln. Learning about the qualities of these great men— courage, honesty, and leadership— can inspire us to do great things with our own lives.   George Washington was the first president of the United States. A famous story says that when George was a little

Teachable Moments

The story of George Washington presents an opportunity to talk about honesty. Make sure your children know that they do not have to be afraid to tell you the truth. They must know both that you will love and forgive them, and that there are sometimes consequences for their actions that cannot be ignored.

boy, he cut down his father's cherry tree with a hatchet. George's father was very angry, and he asked George who had cut the tree down. George told his father, "I cannot tell a lie. I cut down the cherry tree." And George's father forgave him because he told the truth. We don't know if the story of the cherry tree is really true, but we do know that George Washington proved himself to be an honest, trustworthy man.

Cherry Tarts

Things you'll need:

- wax paper
- rolling pin
- 4-inch circle pattern
- knife
- muffin pan
- medium bowl
- spoon
- measuring spoons
- grater
- cherry-shaped cookie cutter or cherry pattern

Ingredients:

- 1 package (2 crusts) prepared pie crust, thawed
- 1 14-ounce can cherry pie filling
- ½ teaspoon vanilla extract
- 1 tablespoon finely grated lemon rind
- 2 tablespoons butter
- 3 tablespoons vanilla sugar*

1. Preheat oven to 350 degrees.

2. Place thawed pie crust on wax paper. Roll with floured rolling pin until all creases are out. Cut four-inch circles in the pie crust.

3. Place pie crust circles in cups of muffin pan that have been sprayed with cooking spray. Then press crusts to form tart shells.

4. In a medium bowl, stir together pie filling, vanilla extract, and grated lemon rind.

5. Place ¼ cup of the mixture into the center of each pie crust circle. Dot each tart with butter.

6. Using the remaining dough, cut out the shape of a cherry with a stem and place on top of each tart.

7. Sprinkle each tart with vanilla sugar and bake for 20 minutes.

For vanilla sugar: Place a vanilla bean and sugar in a tightly closed container a day ahead of time. For stronger flavor, leave bean in sugar longer.

Makes 8 tarts.

Abraham Lincoln's Birthday

 ABRAHAM LINCOLN WAS the sixteenth president of the United States. Everyone has heard about how he loved to read and has heard that he was called "Honest Abe." There is a legend that Abe walked ten miles just to return a library book.

Abe Lincoln grew up in a log cabin in Kentucky. His neighbors recognized his leadership abilities and elected him to the state legislature. Later he was elected to the U.S. House of Representatives.

Lincoln became president during one of the most difficult times in our nation's history. Just a few weeks after he took office, the nation was torn apart in a great civil war between the North and the South, with the two sides divided over slavery. Abraham Lincoln believed that slavery was wrong, and he stood by his belief through a long and terrible war.

Teachable Moments

Pretend with your child that she is the president of the family for a day. Work with her in making decisions that affect the whole family. These might include what to eat at mealtime and what to do for fun before bedtime. Help her consider the needs and interests of everyone in order to make the best decisions.

Abe Lincoln's Log Cabin

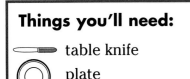
Ingredients:

4 graham crackers
chocolate tube icing
1 small bag thick pretzel sticks
1 plain chocolate bar

1. Using a table knife, carefully cut all graham crackers into squares. Using the chocolate tube icing as "glue," glue four cracker halves into a cube shape.

2. To make a roof, tilt two cracker halves at an angle above the cube and glue with icing. Triangular spaces above cube can be filled with cracker halves cut diagonally.

3. Spread or squeeze icing onto one side of each pretzel stick and place carefully on cabin wall. Cover each side of "cabin" with rows of horizontal pretzel "logs."

4. To make a covering for the roof, break chocolate bar into two large square pieces. Use icing to glue each piece to an opposite side of the roof. Additional icing can be used to add a door or window.

For younger children: House may be made more simply in two-dimensional form on a brightly colored paper plate. Use one graham cracker square for the house shape and one diagonally-cut cracker for the roof. Canned icing may be used instead of a tube.

Makes 1 log cabin.

Independence Day

 INDEPENDENCE DAY, or the Fourth of July, celebrates the signing of the Declaration of Independence. This was a very important event in our nation's history, beginning the struggle to make the United States a free and independent country.

Today, Independence Day is a time for remembering the freedom we have as Americans. It is celebrated by fireworks, picnics, and parades. The red, white, and blue of our American flag are seen everywhere.

This Fourth of July, choose a good book or movie about the signing of the Declaration of Independence. Enjoy it as a family, and talk about the hardships our forefathers experienced to make America free. Then celebrate our freedom by making one of the most traditional American desserts—apple pie!

Teachable Moments

Talk about some of the freedoms our forefathers gained for us— freedom of religion, freedom of speech, freedom of the press. Choose one and think about what your life would be like without it. For example, tell your child what he can and cannot talk about for the rest of the day. This can be a powerful reminder of the value of freedom!

Little Apple Tartlets

Ingredients:

- 1 package (2 crusts) prepared pie crust, thawed
- 3 Granny Smith apples, peeled, cored, and sliced
- ¼ cup brown sugar
- 1 teaspoon cinnamon
- 2 tablespoons brown sugar mixed with ½ teaspoon cinnamon

1. Preheat oven to 350 degrees.

2. Roll pie crusts out to remove the creases and cut four 3-inch squares from crust.

3. Shape each square into a tart crust and place in a small aluminum pie plate or muffin pan. Pierce pie crust with a fork.

4. Bake for five minutes. Cool.

5. In a medium bowl, mix apples, ¼ cup brown sugar, and 1 teaspoon cinnamon until thoroughly combined.

6. Distribute the apple mixture evenly among the cooled pie crusts.

7. With a small star-shaped cookie cutter, cut the remaining pastry into 12 stars.

8. Place three stars on top of the apple mixture on each tartlet. Sprinkle the top with sugar/cinnamon mixture and bake for 15 to 20 minutes, or until golden brown.

Makes 4 tarts.

Kwanza

KWANZA IS A CULTURAL HOLIDAY celebrated December 26 to January 1 by many Black American families and others of African descent. It recognizes and remembers African-inspired culture and values. It is a time for paying respect to past, present, and future Black Americans.

The word *kwanza* means "first fruits of the harvest." The celebration lasts for one week and ends with a ceremony that includes a huge feast. Seven values are emphasized during the Kwanza season: unity, self-determination, cooperation, sharing by all, creativity, purpose, and faith.

Kwanza is full of symbolism and tradition. One of these traditions is the serving of *mazao,* or fruits and vegetables, which stand for the value of working together. Other traditions are sitting on the *mekea,* or straw mat, which represents respect for tradition, and drinking from the *kikombe cha umoja,* which is a unity cup.

Sweet potatoes are a favorite vegetable served during Kwanza. Here is a unique way of preparing them.

Teachable Moments

We live in fast-paced, transient times. Because of this, we are losing the values, traditions, and stories distinctive to our heritage. One of the most important things parents can do for children is to maintain the contact between generations. As you cook together, talk about some things your mother and grandmother used to cook. Ask your child to recall stories she remembers about grandparents or other relatives, and add some of your own.

Sweet Potato Bundles

Things you'll need:

knife
cutting board
skillet
measuring cup
spatula
paper towels

Ingredients:

2 large sweet potatoes, scrubbed
salt
black pepper
1 cup canola oil
green onion tops, optional

1. Peel and cut sweet potatoes lengthwise into strips ¼- to ⅜-inch wide.

2. Toss sweet potatoes with salt and pepper.

3. Place oil in a skillet and heat over medium heat. Carefully place the sweet potatoes in the oil with a spatula.

4. Fry for about eight minutes, turning to cook evenly.

5. Remove and place on paper towels to drain.

6. Serve as is or tie in bundles with tops of green onions.

Serves 4.

My Favorite Recipes

Holidays and Special Days!

Ingredients: _____

_____

_____

_____

_____

_____

_____

_____

_____

_____

Recipe for: _____

From: _____

Notes: _____

My Favorite Recipes

Holidays and Special Days!

Ingredients: _____

_____

_____

_____

_____

_____

_____

_____

_____

Recipe for: _____

From: _____

Notes: _____

My Favorite Recipes

Holidays and Special Days!

Ingredients: _____

_____

_____

_____

_____

_____

_____

_____

_____

_____

Recipe for: _____

From: _____

Comments: _____